SPORTS

j796.3578   Su
Sullivan   c.2
Better softball for
boys and girls

BOOKMOBILE
EXTENSION DEPARTMENT
Syracuse Public Library

Books in This Series

Better Archery for Boys and Girls
Better Baseball for Boys
Better Basketball for Boys
Better Bicycling for Boys and Girls
Better Bowling for Boys
Better Boxing for Boys
Better Camping for Boys
Better Fishing for Boys
Better Football for Boys
Better Golf for Boys
Better Gymnastics for Boys
Better Horseback Riding for Boys and Girls
Better Ice Hockey for Boys
Better Karate for Boys
Better Physical Fitness for Boys
Better Physical Fitness for Girls
Better Sailing for Boys and Girls
Better Scuba Diving for Boys
Better Soccer for Boys
Better Softball for Boys and Girls
Better Surfing for Boys
Better Swimming and Diving for Boys and Girls
Better Table Tennis for Boys and Girls
Better Tennis for Boys and Girls
Better Track and Field Events for Boys
Better Water Skiing for Boys

For his help in the preparation of this book, special thanks are offered Vince Scamardella, ASA Commissioner, Metropolitan New York City. The author is also grateful to Don Porter, Executive Director, ASA; Herb Field, Herb Field Studios; Gary Wagner, Wagner International Photos; Ed Wade, Neil Katine, Lou Reno, Michael Roselle, Tom O'Connor, and Timothy Sullivan. Thanks are also offered these youngsters who served as photographic models: Walter Briggs, Douglas Marshall, Bernie Tortora, Ronald Olsen, Joe and Mike Roselle, and Nancy and Susan Jozwiak.

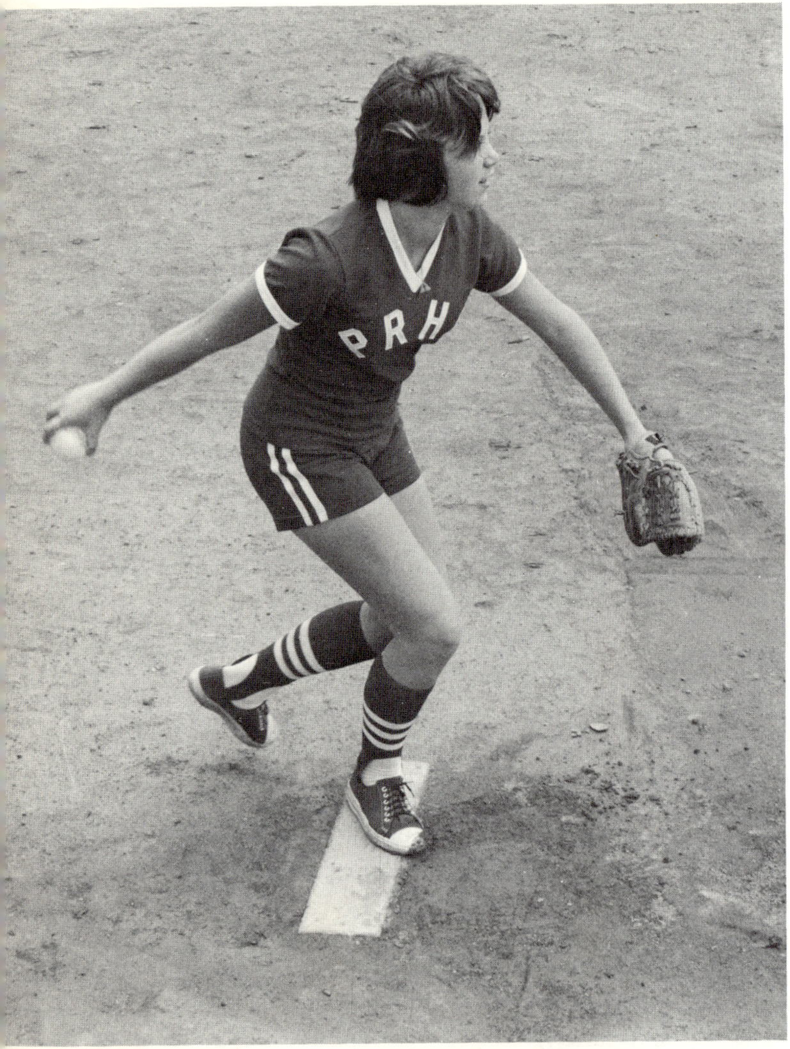
PRH

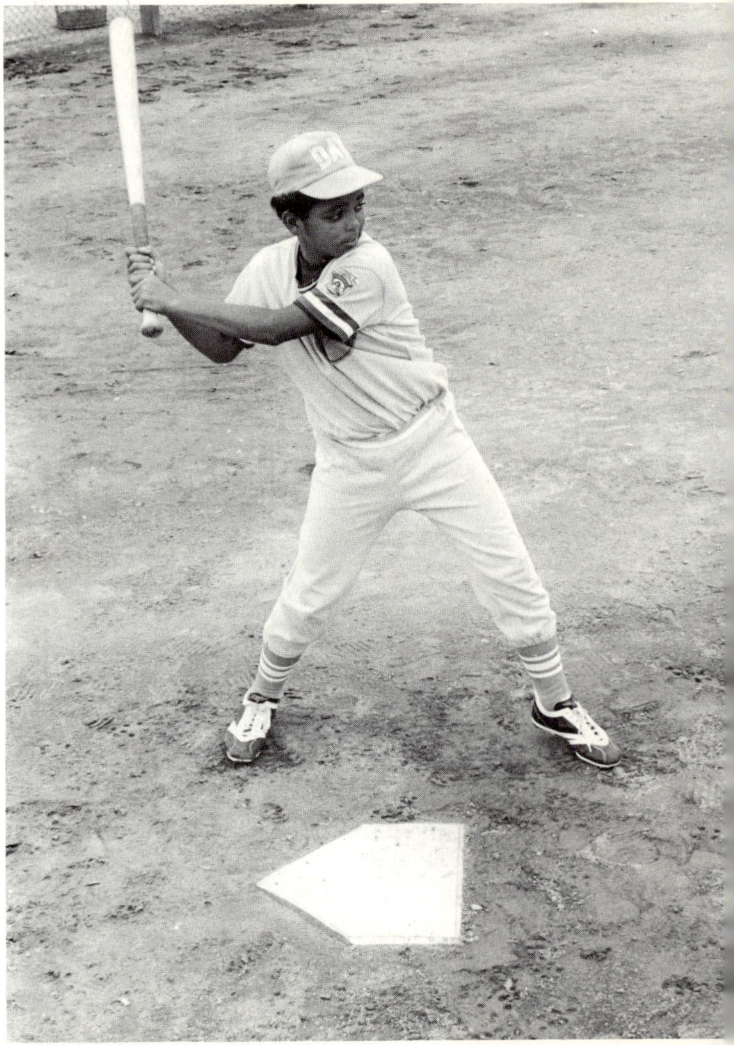

BETTER SOFTBALL
for Boys and Girls

George Sullivan

DODD, MEAD & COMPANY · NEW YORK

PICTURE CREDITS

AMF Voit, 10 (bottom); Hillerich & Bradsby, 11, 12 (left); J. de Beer & Co., 10 (row 2 right, row 3); Rawlings Sporting Goods, 12 (right), 13 (top left); Spalding, 10 (top, row 2 left); Wilson Sporting Goods, 8 (right), 13 (bottom left). All other photographs are by George Sullivan.

Library of Congress Cataloging in Publication Data
Sullivan, George, 1927
   Better softball for boys and girls.
   SUMMARY: Gives instructions in basic softball techniques.
   1. Softball—Juvenile literature. [1. Softball] I. Title.
GV881.S89   796.357'8   74–25507
ISBN 0–396–07063–9

Copyright © 1975 by George Sullivan
All rights reserved
No part of this book may be reproduced in any form
without permission in writing from the publisher
Printed in the United States of America

CONTENTS

Everyone's Game	6	Playing First Base	41
Equipment	10	Playing Shortstop and Second Base	43
How to Hit	15	Playing Third Base	46
How to Bunt	20	Playing the Outfield	48
On the Bases	22	The Short Fielder	56
How to Slide	25	Defensive Teamwork	57
How to Pitch	28	How to Coach	62
Catching	34	Glossary	64
Infield Play	39		

EVERYONE'S GAME

The nice thing about softball is that just about anyone can play the game and excel.

In baseball, the pitcher dominates, and sometimes the hitter never gets to take the bat from his shoulder. Football is for roughnecks. But softball is different. It's a game that stresses having fun.

Softball was first played in 1887. The scene was Chicago, the Farragut Boat Club. George Hancock, a reporter for the Chicago Board of Trade, seeking a baseball-like game that could be played indoors when the weather was mean, took some string and bound up an old boxing glove into a ball shape. Throwing underhand, he hurled this primitive "soft ball" toward a friend who faced him with a broomstick bat. Others joined in and teams were formed.

Hancock later wrote a complete set of rules for the game and developed a special ball and a rubber-tipped bat. From these simple beginnings softball grew into the popular sport it is today.

During the early 1900s, many variations of softball sprang up, and the game came to be known by several different names—mush ball, big ball, kitten ball, and playground ball among them. It wasn't until 1933 that a committee was formed to standardize the playing rules. "Softball" has been the official name of the game since that year.

Another reason that 1933 is important is because it is the year the American Softball Association was formed. The ASA has played a significant role in the sport's growth, not only in the United States but in foreign countries as well. International softball

Whether slow-pitch or fast-pitch, the pitch is underhand.

competition is governed by the International Softball Federation, founded in 1952, and which boasts more than forty member countries.

The rules and regulations that govern softball are the best evidence there is that the game, in its early stages at least, represented an attempt to play baseball indoors. Because of the limited area, the playing field had to be smaller. Because the infielders and outfielders were thus closer to the batter, a softer, more substantial ball had to be used. And the bat had to be made smaller and lighter.

When all of these rules revisions were accomplished, one problem remained: The pitcher was so close to the batter that he had an overwhelming advantage. The rulesmakers sought to restore the balance by making the pitcher throw underhand.

They were only partly successful. Even though they were throwing underhand, pitchers could rocket the ball to the plate at speeds that approached 100 mph. One hitless inning after another was often the result. Pitcher Clarence (Buck) Miller, a member of Softball's Hall of Fame, has 96 no-hit games to his credit. In baseball, Sandy Koufax holds the lifetime record for no-hit games; he has four. Betty Grayson, another Hall of Famer, once recorded a string of 115 scoreless innings. She had an appropriate nickname; she was known as Bullet Betty.

The supremacy that the fast-ball pitcher enjoyed was what led to the development of a second version of the game—slow-pitch softball. Fast-pitch softball was dominant through the 1940s and 1950s (when Buck Miller and Bullet Betty were active), but during the 1960s, slow-pitch came to be more popular. Today about 75 per cent of all games are of the slow-pitch variety.

The rules for slow-pitch softball state that when the pitcher delivers the ball his arm cannot go any higher than hip level. There's no windmilling, in other words, and this serves to reduce the speed of the ball. The rulebook says that the ball must be delivered at a "moderate speed." Excessive speed can be a cause for ejection.

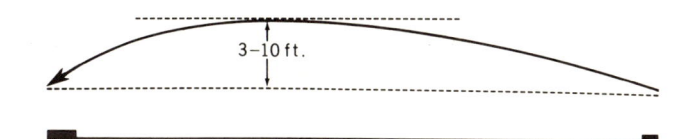

In slow-pitch softball, arc of the ball must be 3 to 10 feet.

The rules for slow-pitch softball also specify what the ball's trajectory is to be. The ball must be delivered so that it traces a banana-shaped arc on its way to the batter. The arc must be at least 3 feet in height, but can be no higher than 10 feet.

All pitching—fast-pitch and slow-pitch—must be underhand. In fast-pitch, the pitcher is allowed to use any motion he wants, providing he does not make more than one revolution of his arm in the course of his delivery.

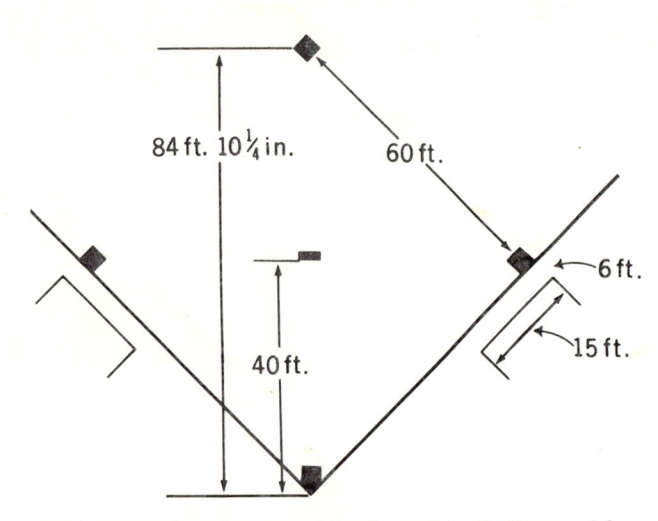

For boys and girls 13 to 18, the softball diamond has these measurements.

An official softball game is seven innings (instead of nine, as in baseball). The ball is 12 inches in circumference.

The size of the playing field is the same for fast-pitch as it is for slow-pitch. For both boys and girls ages 13 to 18, the pitcher stands 40 feet from home plate (instead of 46 feet as in adult play). The bases are 60 feet apart (the same as for adults). For boys and girls ages 9 to 12, the pitching distance is 35 feet. The distance between bases is 45 feet.

The rules further state that "no barrier or fence shall be placed less than 200 feet from home plate."

The coach's box is 15 feet long and 6 feet from the baseline.

Fast-pitch softball teams have nine players, the same nine as a baseball team. In slow-pitch softball, there are ten players to a team. The tenth player is a short fielder. He usually patrols an area behind second base on the outfield grass, but some teams use the short fielder as an outfielder. This gives the team four outfielders: a left fielder, a left center fielder, a right center fielder, and a right fielder.

Slow-pitch rules do not permit bunting or base stealing. In fast-pitch, while baserunners are permitted to steal, their movement is restricted. They are not permitted to take leads off bases, but must keep in contact with the base until the pitch is delivered.

Any junior team registered with the Amateur

Pitcher's plate and home plate look like this.

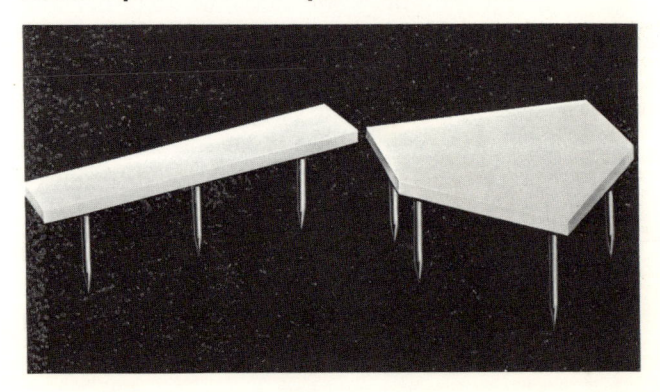

HOME PLATE

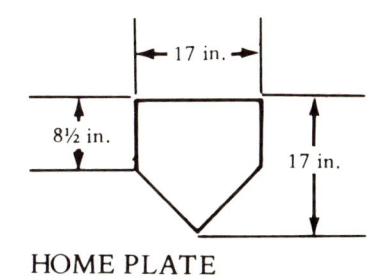

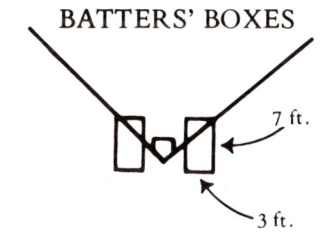

BATTERS' BOXES

PITCHER'S PLATE

Softball Association is eligible to take part in championship competition. For 9-to-12-year-old boys and girls, championship competition does not go beyond the state level, but for older boys and girls there are regional and national tournaments in these divisions:

> 13-15 Girls' Fast Pitch
> 13-15 Girls' Slow Pitch
> 13-15 Boys' Fast Pitch
> 13-15 Boys' Slow Pitch
> 16-18 Girls' Fast Pitch
> 16-18 Girls' Slow Pitch
> 16-18 Boys' Fast Pitch
> 16-18 Boys' Slow Pitch

For more information about tournament competition, write to the American Softball Association (2801 N.E. 50th Street, P. O. Box 11437, Oklahoma City, Oklahoma 73111). A free rulebook is also available from the organization.

Tournament competition is also conducted by the Miss Softball America Foundation (2889 East La Palma, Anaheim, California 92806). In one recent year, more than 10,000 girls in 22 states took part in leagues organized under the Miss Softball America banner.

EQUIPMENT

One of the most appealing features of softball is that the equipment requirements for the game do not place any great demands on one's pocketbook. All you really need to play the game is a softball, a softball bat—the bat being a scaled-down version of the bat used in baseball—and an open field.

The Ball—The name "softball" is something of a misnomer. In an earlier day, the ball was, indeed, soft—as soft as a ripe grapefruit—but not any more. Today's softballs are very hard when they're new, although not rock-hard like baseballs.

In junior play, the ball must be between 11⅞ and 12⅛ inches in circumference. It must weigh between 6 and 6¾ ounces.

Softballs are filled with either cork or rubber or a mixture of both, or with kapok, a silky fiber that is also used as a padding in pillows and mattresses. Strong yarn is wound around the filling, then coated with latex or rubber cement. The outer cover is of tanned cowhide or horsehide, usually the latter.

You won't be involved with the game for very long before you begin to see softballs of many different kinds. Some, instead of having seams flush to the outer covering, as the rulebook specifies, will be "outseamed." Balls of this type are meant for use on cement or asphalt-covered playing fields. Other softballs have a rubber-based covering; they're waterproof.

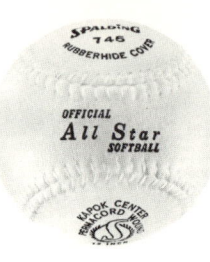

Softballs come in a wide range of styles.

The Bat—Bats for junior play come in a variety of lengths, beginning at 26 inches and ranging in one-inch steps up to 34 inches. The rules say that a bat cannot exceed 34 inches nor be greater than 2½ inches in diameter at its thickest part. (The section in this book titled "How to Hit" explains how to choose a bat that's the right size.)

Bats are available in different styles, too. Style relates to shape. Some have thick handles and barrels; others are slim and whippy; still others have a unique bottle shape. In choosing a bat, the matter of style is much less important than the bat's length and how it "feels" when you swing it.

Some manufacturers offer special bats for girls, which are usually smaller versions of boys' bats. They have such names as "Duchess" and "Lady Luck." Metal bats for girls sometimes come in pastel colors. The reason for doing all of this is questionable. After all, a player should choose a bat on the basis of its particular length, weight, and handle size. A girl doesn't need a special bat any more than she needs a special glove or cap.

Bats can be made of metal or wood, the wood being ash, usually. If you use a wood bat, remember to hold it correctly when you go to the plate. Keep the trademark facing upward. This will position the bat so you will be hitting off the side of the wood grain, which serves to give greater punch to the hit. It also makes it less likely that the bat will crack or splinter.

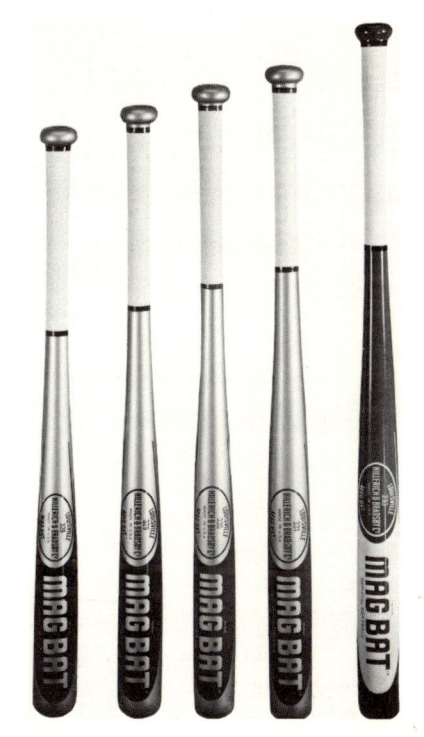

Bats are available in several lengths.

You don't have to worry about cracking or splintering when you use a metal bat. Metal usually means aluminum, although bats are also made of magnesium, said to be superior to aluminum in that it is less susceptible to denting and bending.

Up until fairly recent times, bats were made of wood exclusively. The reason that you now see so

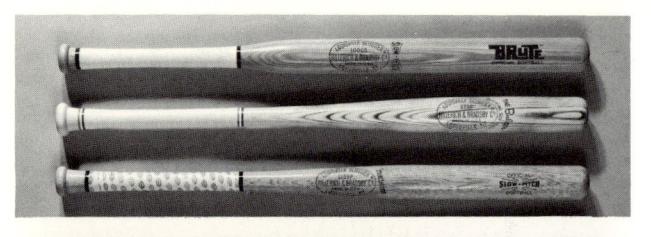

Bats vary in style, too.

many metal bats is largely an economic one. Since metal bats do not break, they can be used season after season, and this represents an important saving to budget-minded athletic directors. It must be said, however, that the initial cost of a metal bat is two or three times that of a wood one.

Bats made of nylon were introduced in the 1970s. They look something like those of wood, but on close examination you'll notice they have a smooth plastic finish. Like aluminum bats, nylon bats are virtually unbreakable.

If you've purchased a bat of your own and plan to tape the handle, keep in mind that this "safety grip," as the rulebook calls it, must extend a minimum of 10 inches from the knob end, and cannot go beyond 15 inches.

Gloves and Mitts—The official rules of softball make a distinction between gloves and mitts. In the case of a glove, there are separate sheaths for each finger and the thumb. With a mitt, there's usually only a sheath for the thumb, although some first basemen's mitts offer a sheath that's big enough to accommodate both the thumb and forefinger. Mitts, says the rulebook, can be worn only by first basemen and catchers.

Modern gloves have deep pockets, and wide and ruggedly-built webbing, which makes trapping the

Gloves need large, deep pockets, wide webbing.

Typical softball mitt

ball much easier than it used to be. But no matter how elaborately your glove is fitted out, learn to use two hands whenever you catch the ball. Attempts at one-handed catches often result in errors. Rub the glove with oil occasionally to keep it soft.

Can you use a baseball glove for softball? Of course; just be sure the pocket is big enough.

Catcher's mask is light in weight, has thick padding.

Girl catchers must wear chest protectors, says rulebook.

Catching Equipment—A catcher must wear a mask, says the rulebook. A catcher's mask has a wire frame, thick vinyl padding, and an adjustable head harness. Girls who serve as catchers, the rules say, must wear chest protectors.

Cleats like these are recommended.

Footwear—There's nothing in the rulebook that says you can't wear baseball-type metal cleats when playing softball; however, most coaches prefer their players to wear shoes with circular molded cleats. They are about equal in the traction they provide and they cause fewer injuries.

Many players, even those who compete in organized leagues and championship tournaments, wear sneakers. The rule to follow is to wear whatever type of footwear enables you to be quick and fast on the playing surface used by your team.

Uniforms—Wear any type of clothing that feels comfortable and allows plenty of freedom of movement. For most teams, the uniform consists of a T-shirt with the team name printed across the front, a peaked cap, jeans, and sneakers.

For championship competition, a complete uniform is mandatory. This consists of a cap, socks, a shirt or blouse, and pants. The pants are usually the knicker-type, as worn in baseball. Girls' teams often wear shorts. The Oklahoma City Cobras did when they won the National Girls Slow Pitch championship recently.

Choking up on the bat is likely to help your swing.

HOW TO HIT

Softball, much more than baseball, is a game of line drives, of base hits that are lashed just beyond the infielders' reach, whether on the ground or in the air.

To hit line drives, what you need is an easy, natural swing. A furious swing, a home-run swing, causes problems.

This is much more true in softball than in baseball. Because the ball is bigger and the bat thinner, you have to contact the ball almost dead center in order to be successful. Hit high on the ball and you'll top it; a weak dribbler will be the result. Hit low on the ball and you'll pop it up for an easy out.

"What's the most important piece of advice you have for the batter?" I asked several coaches. Each had about the same answer: "Swing easy; don't try to kill the ball."

Pick out a bat that feels comfortable for you, one that you can grip firmly, one that you can swing effortlessly. No one is going to argue with the fact that the heavier the bat, the farther it can whack the ball. But the extra weight of the heavy bat isn't going to help you unless you can whip it around. So follow this general rule: Use the heaviest bat that you can swing with ease.

It doesn't make much difference whether you use a bat that's made of wood or one of metal. Each type is available in a wide range of lengths, weights, and handle sizes.

Some players prefer wood bats because they feel they have a whippiness, a snap, and this enables them to hit the ball with greater authority. Others say that metal bats give more solid hits. It's really a matter of personal preference. Use whichever type gives you a feeling of confidence.

You can grip the bat in either one of two different ways—with your lower hand up against the knob at the handle end, or with the hands a few inches from the knob, what's called a choke-up grip.

Choking up on the bat is common in softball,

especially in the fast-pitch version of the game. When a batter chokes up, he's able to get the bat around much faster and, thus, better able to punch or slap the ball over the heads of the infielders. It's also easier to place the ball.

Whatever style you use, keep your hands together on the bat. Grip firmly but don't let your fingers

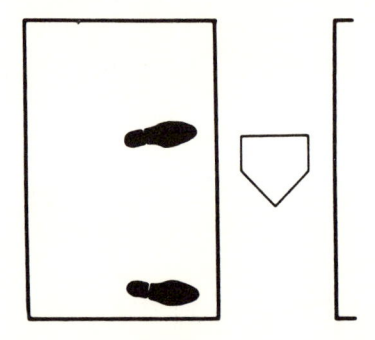

Coaches recommend either the square stance (top) or open stance.

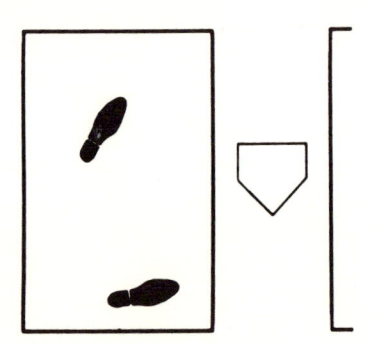

tighten or become tense. If you do, you won't be able to swing hard.

Choose a type of stance that feels natural. There are three types: open, closed, and square.

In the square stance, both feet are the same distance from the edge of the plate. In the closed stance, the front foot is closer to the plate.

You're likely to have the best results if you use an open stance, one in which the front foot is drawn farther away from the plate than the rear one. Not only will a stance of this type enable you to follow the pitch with greater ease, but it will help you to get the bat around quickly. Of course, you can't permit your stance to become too open. If you do, you won't be able to reach pitches on the outside corner of the plate.

Don't take your turn at bat without having a mental image of the area embraced by the strike zone. The rulebook defines the strike zone as "that space over home plate which is between the batter's armpits and the top of his knees." As this suggests, the strike zone is 17 inches wide (the width of the plate) and rectangular in shape, the height of the rectangle depending on the batter's size.

The hitters with the highest averages seldom swing at pitches outside their strike zones. "There's no sense to it," says a Clifton, New Jersey, teen-ager. "If the pitcher thinks he can get you to swing at a bad pitch, you'll never see a good one."

The umpire defines each batter's strike zone on

Know your strike zone; it's the area the width of the plate between the top of the knees and the armpits.

the basis of what the rulebook calls a normal stance. This means that if you crouch down in an effort to compress the size of the strike zone, the idea being to draw a base on balls, the strategy isn't likely to be successful. It's your normal stance that the umpire will use.

Take some practice swings before you step into the batter's box. They'll help you to relax.

Get comfortable at the plate. Your feet should be about shoulder-width apart. Your weight should be evenly distributed on the balls of your feet.

There's no need to crouch down. Sink in your knees a bit, but stay fairly erect.

Cock the bat behind your right ear (if you're a right-handed batter). Hold the arms away from your body. The right elbow should point toward the ground.

Now the pitcher gets set. Concentrate, not on the pitcher, but on the ball. From the time it leaves the pitcher's hand, keep your eyes glued on it. Follow it right up until the instant it strikes the bat.

As the pitcher goes into his delivery, shift your weight to your rear foot and cock the bat a little bit more. Tighten your grip. Imagine your body to be like a spring at this stage, compressing before its power is released.

You want to try to meet the ball out in front of the plate. So stride forward with the front foot, and then whip the bat around. Keep your hands about chest high. Keep your hips and shoulders level—so you'll have a level swing.

Striding forward helps you to get your hips into the swing, which assures power. It doesn't have to be a long stride. Six inches is about right, certainly no more than eight inches. And you don't have to lift your foot high off the ground when you stride. It's a short step; it's a low step.

After making contact with the ball, pull the bat around. Never stop your swing short. The wrists roll over during this phase, the right wrist rolling over the left. The bat ends up behind your back.

Remember to keep your head still. If you jerk your head in one direction or another, your eyes have to refocus on the ball, and this disrupts your timing.

Don't try to outguess the pitcher as you await the throw. Figure a fastball is coming. Then if it's a drop or a change-up, you have a chance to adjust mentally, then swing accordingly. But if you are looking for an off-speed pitch, and the fastball comes in, it can zip right by you before you can get the bat around.

Cock the bat as you await the pitch; stride and swing; follow through.

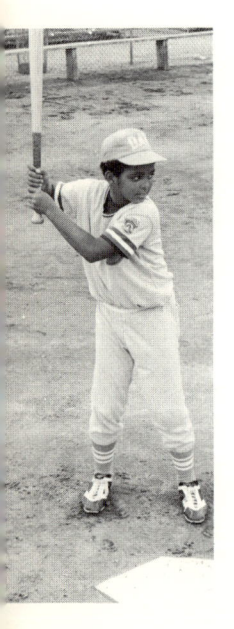

As a hitter in slow-pitch softball, you don't have to be concerned about the speed of the pitch. But you do have to be able to judge the ball's trajectory, and decide how high the ball is going to be when it enters the strike zone. A pitch that is dropping groundward as it approaches you can be a ball when it comes to your front shoulder, but a strike by the time it reaches your rear shoulder.

The matter of whether you should swing at a particular pitch depends on many factors. If your team is trailing by three or four runs, it's usually best to take the first pitch. You have to do all you possibly can to get on base, to trigger a rally that is going to provide your team with a bunch of runs. Also take the first pitch any time the pitcher is having problems with his control. If everyone on the team does this, it forces the pitcher to make extra pitches, which are likely to add to his woe.

These tips usually don't apply, however, if you come to the plate with runners in scoring position. Then you'll want to swing at the first pitch that looks good to you.

If you're experienced as a hitter, look for an opportunity to place your hits. For example, if the short fielder is playing you as a pull hitter, maybe you can slam the ball over second base. If you're a right-handed hitter and the right fielder has moved close to second base, maybe you can close up your stance and rap the ball down the right-field line.

"I love to see the third baseman move in close when I come to the plate," says a young pull hitter from Bristol, Connecticut. "I open up my stance even more and try to slam the ball right at him. I know he'll never be able to handle the ball cleanly enough to make the throw."

How to Practice—A simple backyard drill will help you improve as a hitter. You need an area that's about 30 feet by 10 feet. For equipment, you need a batting tee and a supply of plastic balls, equipment that can be purchased in virtually any sporting goods store.

String a net or blanket between two poles. Its upper edge should be about 8 feet above the ground. Set up the batting tee about 20 feet from the net. Adjust the height of the tee so you will, with a level swing, hit line drives.

Take ten swings and see how many times you can put the ball into the net. If the ball goes over the net or bounces on the ground before reaching it, it's a sign you're not hitting dead center.

Another good way to practice is to swing a bat at home in front of a full-length mirror. As you take your stance, check your shoulders to see that they are level and that your arms are away from your body. As you swing, check to see that the bat is level and you're keeping your head steady.

If you're a member of a team, you'll be taking part in batting practice sessions. Use them to improve your timing. Concentrate on drilling each pitch up the middle.

HOW TO BUNT

In fast-pitch softball, bunting is a vital skill. If you can't bunt successfully, there are times when you are going to hurt your team.

Not in slow-pitch, however. If you bunt in slow-pitch, you're automatically out.

There are two types of bunts. There's the sacrifice bunt, in which you advance a baserunner by forcing the infield to retire you at first base; you "sacrifice" your time at bat, in other words. The other type is the bunt for a base hit, usually called a drag bunt.

When attempting a sacrifice bunt, turn your body so as to face the pitcher squarely, crouching slightly. Slide your upper hand up the bat and grasp lightly at a point near the trademark, the thumb on top, the fingers underneath. The other hand grips at the handle end. Keep the bat parallel to the ground.

The whole idea is to simply deaden the speed of the pitch by allowing the bat to absorb the impact of the ball. That's why a *loose* grip is important. Grip tightly and the ball will rebound to one of the infielders, and maybe they'll nail the baserunner.

You don't have to swing. You don't have to push at the ball. And don't pull the bat back. Just hold it out there as if you were going to catch the ball with it.

To bunt, just hold the bat so that it meets the ball.

Keep the bat perfectly level. If the pitch is higher than you expected, stand more erect to meet it. If it's lower, sink in the knees. What you shouldn't do is tilt the bat. As soon as contact is made, fly toward first base.

When do you execute a sacrifice bunt? It depends on the score, the inning, and other factors, of course, but generally it's used in a close game when there is one out or no outs and a runner is on first base. Your team is trying to get a runner in scoring position. The sacrifice bunt can also be used when there are runners on first and second and your coach is seeking to avoid a double play.

The most effective sacrifice bunts are those that take advantage of potential weak spots in the defense. Suppose there are runners on first and second and none out, and you are called on to execute a sacrifice bunt. Try to place it toward third base. When the third baseman comes in to field the ball, he leaves the base unguarded, so there's no chance that your lead runner will draw a throw.

The squeeze bunt is a type of sacrifice bunt. The game is in a late inning. The score is tied or your team is trailing by a run. There's less than two outs. There's a runner on third. At the instant the ball leaves the pitcher's hand, the runner on third base charges for the plate.

The batter bunts. As the pitcher and an infielder scramble for the ball, the runner crosses the plate. The batter usually gets thrown out at first base.

Poor bunters are seldom used on the squeeze play because a bunt attempt that goes awry can be very costly. If the batter misses the ball, the runner racing in from third is a simple put-out for the catcher. He runs right into the tag. A soft pop-up is even worse. Usually the pitcher grabs it, then tosses to the third baseman for a double play.

Bunting for a base hit requires a different set of techniques than the sacrifice bunt. The idea here is to catch the infielders off guard. The batter pretends he's going to be swinging away. Not until the ball nears the plate does he go into his bunting stance.

Hold the bat more firmly than in the case of a sacrifice. Again, slide the upper hand up the bat toward the trademark. Try to push the ball down one of the baselines, or past the pitcher on his right or left.

There's no need to keep the bat level. Angle it so that the ball will carom away in the direction you

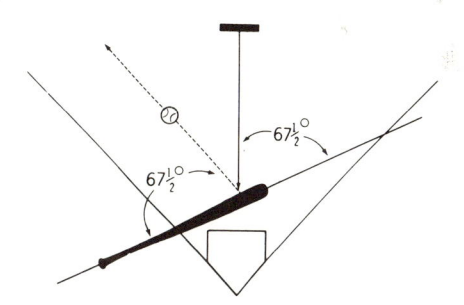

The ball will leave the bat at the same angle it strikes it.

want. Keep in mind that the ball always leaves the bat at the very same angle it strikes it. Try to make contact with the ball at a point about midway between the trademark and the bat's butt end.

Getting away fast is critical. You should actually be on your way toward first base at the time the ball strikes the bat.

If you're a right-handed batter, draw your right foot back as the ball comes toward you. Push off on your left foot as the ball makes contact.

Left-handed batters have an advantage in that they are a full step closer to first base. What the leftie should do is pivot on the ball of his right foot and, with his left, take a crossover step toward first base.

A right-handed batter should try to push the ball down the third base line or try to nudge it toward first base. Lefties can increase their advantage by dumping the ball down the first base line.

ON THE BASES

Being fast is the greatest asset you can have when running the bases, but the ability to think quickly and slide deceptively are almost as important.

Learn to be a canny runner. It will make you a step or two faster in covering the 60 feet between bases. Let's say you're at the plate and you have just poked the ball up the middle. Take your first step with your rear foot. It doesn't make any difference whether you're a right-handed or left-handed batter. Stepping off on the rear foot, by giving you a longer first step, assures you the fastest start possible.

As you dash toward first base, run like a sprinter. Run on your toes. Reach out on each stride. Lift your knees high. Lean forward. Swing your arms at your sides; don't pump them back and forth across your chest.

Keep your head up. If you tuck your chin to your chest, you won't be able to see the play.

If you're trying to beat out an infield hit, run at full throttle right over the base. Don't leap at the bag. Don't attempt to slide into it. Just run.

Many young players make the mistake of running past the base, up the foul line, and into short right field. Instead, you should hold up after you've crossed the base on a hit, and keep alert for a wild throw that could permit you to go to second.

If the ball goes into the outfield and there's a

Left: **When trying to beat out an infield hit, run straight across the base.**

Above: **Hit the base's inside edge as you go by.**

chance you can take an extra base, take a turn toward second. Instead of running arrow-straight for first, veer to your right as you approach the base, and make your turn. By the time you reach first base, you should just about be heading in the direction of second. Touch the inside edge of first base with either foot.

The important thing is to run at full speed. Don't break stride. Once you've made the turn, decide whether you're going all the way to second.

If you do make the turn, keep in mind that you can be tagged out. However, if you merely run straight across first and make no move toward second, the rules say you can't be put out.

Round second base in the same fashion. Swing to your right as you approach it; touch the base on its inside edge. Once you're past second, watch the third base coach for a signal.

In slow-pitch, of course, you can't advance from one base to the next until the ball is hit. In fast-pitch, however, you are permitted to advance as soon as the ball leaves the pitcher's hand. You can also dart for the next base should the ball slip from the pitcher's grip during the windup.

Any time you're on third base and there are less than two outs, be alert for an opportunity to tag up and score. This will occur on a fair fly which is caught. The rules say that you can break for home plate after the catch. This applies in both the slow-pitch and fast-pitch versions of the game.

Rely on the instructions of the third base coach when you tag up. Once you see that a fly ball has been hit, put one foot on the base edge and stretch the other toward home plate. Don't take a long stride. A step the length of a normal walking step is sufficient. Don't follow the flight of the ball; instead, look down the basepath toward home. As soon as the coach yells "Go!" step off the rear foot and dash for the plate.

If it's only a short fly, one on which you cannot reach the plate safely, at least fake a run for the plate, so as to draw a throw from the outfielder. A poor throw or one that eludes the catcher may give you a chance to score.

If you're on third base and there's another runner on first, try to score on a ground ball. If the throw is to the catcher at home plate, and he is waiting there for you to arrive, pull up and force a rundown. This enables the other runners to advance to second and third.

Follow this policy any time you get caught between bases. Not only does it give the other baserunners a chance to advance, it forces the opposition to throw, thereby increasing the chances they'll make an error.

If another runner is coming toward the plate after you've scored, be his coach. Turn and signal him as to whether he should slide. Get the bat and mask out of the runner's way.

As a baserunner, it's part of your responsibility to always know the inning, the number of outs, the count, and, of course, the score. If you're not sure of any of these, call time out and check with a coach or an umpire.

The Hit-and-Run—A team can get greater-than-normal value from a baserunner by using the hit-and-run play. As soon as the ball is released, the runner on first base breaks for second. It looks like an attempted steal, so the second baseman (or shortstop, if a left-handed hitter is at the plate) darts over to take the catcher's throw. The batter swings, driving the ball through the hole created when the infielder vacated his position.

The signal for the hit-and-run is given by the third base coach. Since the idea is to hit the ball to

When you're at third base and planning to tag up, the coach will tell you when to go.

the right side of the infield, the play is usually executed when there's a left-handed hitter at the plate.
Stealing—If you're on first base, you're not likely to get a signal to steal unless there are two outs. The coach reasons that a single is likely to score you from second base, while it will take an extra-base hit to get you home from first. Thus, stealing second is worth the risk.

But there's no sense in stealing third with two outs. On a solid hit, a runner can score from second base almost as readily as he can score from third.

The best time to steal third is with one out. If you're successful, there's a chance you can then score on an infield hit, an infield error, a long fly, or a squeeze bunt.

What about stealing home? Forget it. It should only be tried under what one coach calls "extraordinary circumstances," and then only with two outs.

A double steal is sometimes attempted when there are runners on first and second, or first and third. With the runners on first and second, both men break with the pitch. With runners on first and third, the strategy is different. The man on first goes with the pitch, keeping an eye on the catcher as he runs. If he sees that he can beat the throw, he keeps racing for the bag and slides in. But if the runner believes that the throw is going to nail him, he holds up, thus forcing the infielders to run him down. This is likely to give the man on third an opportunity to break for the plate and score.

HOW TO SLIDE

There are several ways to slide, but the hook slide is the method most coaches recommend. There are two reasons for sliding into a base: To evade the infielder who is about to catch the ball, and to stop your forward progress without having to slow down or break stride. In both instances, the hook slide gets very high marks.

Sometimes the hook slide is called the fall-away slide. As it's being executed, the idea is to lean, or "fall," away from the tag, "hooking" the base with the instep of your extended foot.

Suppose you're sliding to the right, the right side of the base as you approach it. This means that you'll be hooking the base with your left foot.

Don't jump for the base; go into the slide easily, letting the right hip absorb the impact. Bend the right knee; keep the left leg more extended. Both feet should be several inches off the ground so your spikes won't catch.

Lean your upper body away from the base as you near it, and reach out with your left foot so that you make contact with your left instep. Your momentum is likely to carry you right past the base, which is all right. Just keep your foot hooked in place.

Some players slide in the manner described above, but reach out with one hand to evade tag and hook the base. Coaches would rather you hooked with

With the hook slide, the idea is to lean away from the base, hooking it with one foot.

foot as you come into the base.

One advantage of the bent-leg slide is that it permits you to rise to a standing position quickly in the event there's an opportunity to continue to the next base. After making contact with the front foot, you simply lean forward, push off on the other knee, using the momentum of the slide to bring you to your feet.

your foot, however. If you miss the base with a hand hook, you're almost certain to be tagged out. But if you miss with your foot, you can sometimes reach and get it with your hand. You have a backup system, in other words.

While the hook slide may be the recommended method of sliding, it's not the most popular. The bent-leg slide, sometimes referred to as the straight-in slide, is. It's the easiest, most natural way to slide.

You slide directly into the base. Take off and absorb the impact with your hip, the right hip, let's say. Bend your right leg under you. You'll be sliding on the leg and hip.

Extend the left leg. Make contact with the left

You can also go feet first into a base while sliding on your backside. But this method has the disadvantage of giving the baseman a big target—your two feet—to tag.

You can slide on your belly, too, extending your arms and reaching for the base with one hand or both of them. Coaches—and parents—discourage this method for reasons of safety. It puts your head in a danger zone, in the area where the ball is about to arrive.

The safest way to slide is to go feet first, either

The bent-leg slide is the more popular type. It involves sliding straight in to the base.

hooking the base or sliding straight in. To avoid injury to your fingers, keep them cupped as you run and slide. Some players try this trick: While on first base, they pick up a small amount of sand in each hand, and then clench the sand tightly as they run. It's a way of reminding yourself to keep your hands closed.

Many injuries to the feet or ankles that occur while sliding are caused by indecision. A player makes up his mind to slide, but just as he's about to go down he sees that he's got the throw beaten, so he tries to hold up. His feet become entangled with the base as a result, and he ends up wrenching an ankle—or worse. Sliding is an all-or-nothing piece of business. Either do it or don't. And once you've made your mind up, don't change it.

In your first attempts at sliding, you'll probably be content with reaching the base and merely hoping you won't be called out. You can increase your chances of reaching it safely by watching the fielder's glove as he awaits the throw. Aim your tag so that you make contact with the base on the side opposite the glove.

Practice sliding as often as you can. A sliding pit isn't difficult to make. About all you need is a shovel and a level piece of ground. Dig out an area that measures 6 feet by 12 feet and is 18 inches deep. Fill it with fine sand. When you practice sliding, keep a garden rake handy to keep the sand smooth.

HOW TO PITCH

It doesn't matter whether you hurl for a slow-pitch or fast-pitch team; what's important in pitching is coordinating your footwork with the delivery of the ball. You must get your legs and hips into the pitch. Otherwise, it's just an ordinary underhand throw.

In slow-pitch softball, the delivery is a simple back-and-forth motion, something like the delivery a bowler uses in rolling a ball down the lane. The rules say that in neither the backswing nor the forward swing can the ball go higher than your hip.

Hold the ball in both hands. Face the batter squarely. Relax.

Place the front spike of your right foot, your pivot foot, over the edge of the rubber. Angle it a bit so it grips firmly. Keep your other foot a few inches to the rear.

Once you've gotten the signal from the catcher, shift the ball to your right hand, start your arm in motion, and begin your pivot. Keep your eyes on your target, the catcher's mitt.

Stride directly toward the batter. Time the ball's release so that it occurs simultaneously with the shift of your weight from the pivot foot to the front foot.

The rulebook sets down several "don'ts" concern-

The secret of successful pitching is coordinating your footwork with the delivery of the ball.

ing the pitcher's windup. You're not allowed to continue your armswing after you've completed your pivot step. You can't deliberately cause the ball to bounce. And you can't "quick pitch," that is, deliver the ball before the batter has taken his stance.

Control is vital to your success. Unless you can put eight pitches out of ten through the strike zone—the area between the batter's armpits and the top of his knees—you're going to experience many an unhappy afternoon.

Control is a matter of concentration and consistency. As you get set to pitch, concentrate on the mitt target offered by the catcher. Wipe everything else out of your mind.

Being consistent involves developing a smooth, rhythmic delivery, one that enables you to throw pitch after pitch in exactly the same manner. You have to be machine-like.

Keep cool no matter what happens. You can't control your pitches if you let base hits or errors upset you. Take your time. If you feel yourself getting tense, pause for a moment; walk around on the mound until you cool off.

Control problems are sometimes caused because the pitcher fails to release the ball properly. He cups it, in which case the fingers cause the ball to veer off course. Always open up your hand when you deliver, unless you're attempting some type of trick pitch.

Sometimes control problems can be overcome by adjusting your position in relation to the rubber, or pitcher's plate. If you're throwing too far to the outside (to right-handed batters), move slightly to the right on the rubber. Move left if you're throwing too far inside.

If you can't seem to get the ball down, try lengthening your stride. If you're wild low, shorten your stride.

Once you're able to put the ball into the strike zone, you can then work on varying your pitches with the strike. For instance, it's usually best to keep the ball high and inside to a power hitter.

Also learn to vary the time you take between pitches. On one pitch, fire the ball as soon as the

One method of gripping for the change-up

batter gets set. On the very next pitch, make him wait. The rules give you a good deal of leeway in this regard. They say that you can hold the ball anywhere from one second—you *must* hold it one second—to twenty seconds.

In slow-pitch softball, it's not easy to put "stuff" on the ball. Perhaps you can manage some spin, but getting the ball to hook or curve, rise or drop, is a different matter.

What you can do, however, is vary the ball's speed—throw a change-up.

When delivering a change-up, don't vary your windup. If the batter gets any clue that you're throwing a change-up, he can adjust his timing and tee off on the pitch. This is especially true in the case of a poor hitter. Batters who are weak at the plate feast on change-ups.

There are several ways to deliver the change-up. One method calls for you to take a five-fingered grip on the ball, your thumb and forefinger running along the seams. You don't have to grip tightly.

Maintain this five-finger grip until the point of release. At that instant, straighten your three middle fingers so that only your thumb and little finger are in contact with the ball. This type of release works to retard the ball's spin and speed.

Some pitchers use a knuckle-ball type grip when delivering the change-up. They dig the fingernails of two or more fingers into the ball's cover, then snap those fingers straight as they release the ball. Obviously, it's not a grip for beginners.

Before you pitch in a game or for a practice session, take plenty of time to warm up. Do your warm-up throwing over the normal pitching distance —40 feet. Start with easy tosses and increase your speed gradually. Don't throw aimlessly. The catcher should give you a target on every throw.

Once you've warmed up and your control seems to be in hand, start varying your pitches. Practice pitches of varying speeds.

Once the game is underway, warm up at the beginning of each inning. The rules give you one minute to deliver five warmup tosses. Be sure your catcher gives you a target on each one. Throw at medium speed.

Try to make your first pitch a strike to each batter. If you get ahead of the batter by a count of

0-2 or 1-2, try to make him hit at a bad pitch. But don't make it *too* bad. Aim it just outside the strike zone.

Don't concentrate on your delivery and release to such an extent that you overlook your responsibilities as a fielder. Your delivery should be such that as you release the ball you're in a position to field the ball, able to go either to your left or right with equal facility.

On ground balls hit to your left, be ready to cover first base. The first baseman will shout whether you should field the ball or cover the base. On bunts or tricklers in front of the plate, the catcher is the key man. He may wave you away or shout for you to take the ball.

When throwing to a base, pivot quickly and throw deliberately. Never hurry a throw. Keep the ball about chest-high to the player covering the base. When there are runners on base, remember to cover the plate should the pitch get away from the catcher. Also cover the plate on rundowns between third and home.

Fast-Pitch Delivery—When pitching in fast-pitch play, the rules specify that only one arm revolution is permitted. You can't stand on the mound and spin your arm around and around like a propeller blade. Just once.

Most fast-pitch hurlers, after they've acquired some experience, settle upon one of two different windup styles, the windmill or the slingshot. The windmiller faces the batter squarely, his arm and hand in full view of the batter as they whirl through the delivery.

The slingshot is more deceptive. Again the pitcher strides toward the batter, but this time he turns his body to one side, and instead of coming straight through with the ball, he loops it behind his back before releasing it.

Several trick pitches are possible in the fast-pitch version of the game. The change-up (see above) is extremely effective. Fast-pitcher hurlers also employ the rise and drop.

The rise ball, as its name implies, breaks on an upward plane as it nears the batter. While there are several methods of delivering the rise, it's usually done with a two-finger grip, the forefinger running along a seam.

Grip for the rise. Hand turns over; ball spins off the fingertips.

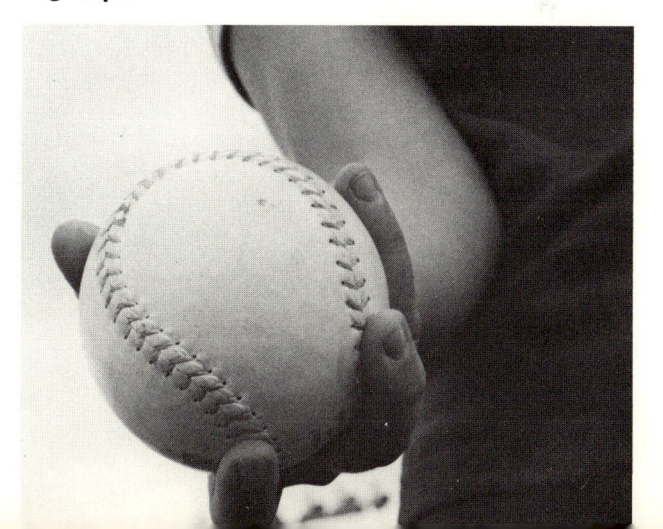

You can also grip like this.

As the arm whirls through the delivery, turn the wrist so that the palm will face the ground at the time of release. In other words, as the fingers are traveling upward, they face downward. And so, as the ball leaves the finger tips, it has a reverse spin, a backward spin. This makes it break in an upward direction.

Rise has reverse spin, breaks upward.

Usually a pitcher will try to keep the rise ball high, aiming it at either the inside or outside corner of the plate. A rise that comes in high and inside is a very difficult pitch to hit.

Most pitchers use the same grip for the drop as they do for the rise. The difference is in the release, the fingers face upward for a drop. This gives the

Drop spins forward, breaks down.

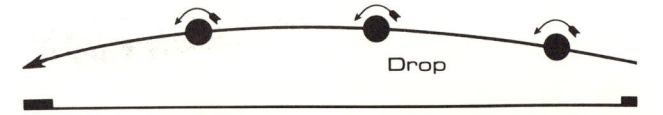

ball a forward spin, the reason it breaks down. Keep the ball low. The drop is very effective inside at the knees.

How to Practice—Practice control every chance you get. Forget about speed. Forget about spin or getting the ball to rise or drop. First learn control; then you can begin to work on some of the subtleties of the art.

Work with your team's catcher. Each time you throw to him, have him give you a target with his mitt. Have him vary the target, positioning it high in the strike zone one time, low the next. Have him move it inside and outside.

If you don't have a catcher to throw to, you can practice control by painting the outline of a strike zone on a cellar wall or the side of a building. When you pitch, the ball will rebound to you. Or, using chalk, you can draw a strike zone on a sheet of canvas or even a blanket. Hang it against the wall or drape it over the clothesline.

Another way to practice is by setting up pitching "strings" that represent the strike zone.

The first step is to make a home plate out of scrap wood. See the section in this book titled "Everyone's Game" for plate dimensions. Paint the plate white. Anchor it in the ground with long spikes.

A pair of posts should be sunk into the ground on either side of the plate. They should be 6 feet tall and spaced 10 feet apart. The forward plane of the posts should line up with the plate's front edge.

String two lengths of heavy twine between the posts. The top string should be at armpit level to a batter of average size. The bottom string should be just above knee level.

Then tie two vertical lengths of twine between the horizontal lengths. These should be as far apart as the width of the plate—17 inches.

Now measure off a distance of 40 feet, from the front edge of the plate, and there establish your pitcher's plate, often called the pitcher's rubber. This can be made out of wood, too, and anchored in the ground with spikes. It should be 6 inches wide, 24 inches long, and 3 or 4 inches thick. The top of the plate should be level with the ground.

Now all you need is someone to catch your practice throws. See how many consecutive pitches you can put through the strings. Once you've achieved some consistency, the next step is to learn to pitch to "spots," to particular sections of the strike zone. Try putting a few throws into the lower left-hand corner of the string rectangle, which would be an outside pitch across the knees (to a right-handed batter). Try hitting the upper right-hand corner, an inside, shoulder-high pitch.

When giving the sign, place your mitt on your knee to conceal the signal from the opposition.

CATCHING

The catcher is second only to the pitcher in importance. He directs the team's defense, and, along with the pitcher, sets pitching strategy. Just as important, the catcher is the team's "holler guy," the player who inspires all others.

Alertness and agility are important in order to be successful as a catcher. It also takes stamina, for you have to be able to withstand the rigors of being in a squatting position for long periods of time.

Your first task as a catcher is to give the pitcher the sign. Squat down; keep your feet fairly close together, your weight concentrated on the balls of your feet. Spread your knees.

Before giving the sign, place your mitt hand at your left knee to conceal the signal from the third base coach. Give the signal with the fingers of the right hand, holding them against the inside of the right thigh. Since you're concealing the signals from the opposition, there's no need to make them complicated. One finger can be used for a fastball; two fingers for a drop; three for a change of pace, and perhaps a fist for a pitchout.

After you've given the sign, rise to a semicrouch, keeping your left foot slightly ahead of your right. You're better able to throw or make a fielding play from this position. Get as close to the batter as you can without endangering yourself from the bat's swing.

Now give the pitcher a target with your mitt, holding it about chin high. Place your bare hand to the right of the mitt; make a fist. This helps to prevent the fingers from being injured.

Whenever the pitch is a strike, make the catch at about belt level. Let the mitt hand "give" a little to cushion the ball's impact.

Any pitch in the strike zone or above it should be caught with the mitt pointing upward. Low pitches should be handled with the mitt down. Very low pitches, those that strike the ground, should be blocked, either with the mitt or your body.

Learn to shift your body when catching pitches

Catching high and low pitches.

Giving the pitcher a mitt target.

Catcher's throw is a snap throw, the ball delivered from behind the right ear with a quick wrist snap.

outside of the strike zone. Get in front of the ball. When the pitch is high, stand almost erect; for a low pitch, go down on your right knee. On a pitch that is inside (to a right-handed batter), step to the left with your left foot. To glove an outside pitch, step to the right with your right foot. No matter how you stride, always remember to keep your left foot slightly ahead of your right, so you can get the throw away quickly.

The catcher's throw is a snap throw. There's no windup. Simply take the ball back and whip it overhand toward the target, using quick forearm and wrist action. You should be able to make the catch and shift into throwing position with fluid speed.

When you make the throw, target on the edge of the base nearest the oncoming runner. Keep the ball at about knee level. Don't hold your throw, waiting for the infielder to get to the base. It's his responsibility to arrive there before the ball does.

Most of your throws will go to second base but there are exceptions. Suppose there are runners on first and third, a double-steal is called. Where do you throw? You can throw toward second base and have the pitcher cut it off, then rifle the ball back to you. Or you can bluff a throw to second, then throw to the third baseman, the idea being to catch the lead runner in a rundown.

Calling the Pitches—It's up to you to study the batter—the way he grips the bat, his stance, his stride, and swing—and call the appropriate pitches. Generally, what you must try to do is keep the ball away from the hitter's power. With a pull hitter at the plate, a batter using an open stance, keep the ball inside. Pitch him on the fists; jam him.

A batter with a quick swing is always a big problem. Usually he feasts on fastballs. Keep the speed down and try feeding him pitches that are low and outside. Call for low pitches in the case of a batter who stands erect.

If a batter seems eager to hit, slow down the pace. Make him wait by delaying the flashing of the sign.

What about a weak hitter? If your pitcher has a good fastball, try to strike the man out. Or call for a rise and make him pop up.

The game situation can affect the kind of pitch you ask for. With a runner on first and less than two out, you should try to force the batter to hit on the ground by calling for pitches at his knees. In a sacrifice situation, with the batter eager to bunt, call for pitches at armpit level.

Handling Pop-ups—High pops, in fair territory or foul, shouldn't be any problem, if you remember a few pointers. A right-handed batter will almost always foul an outside pitch to your right and an inside pitch to your left. With a left-handed batter, the opposite applies.

In going after a pop-up, slide the mask over your head but don't discard it until you've located the ball. Toss it in the opposite direction. The same holds true when you're fielding a bunt.

When pursuing a pop-up, get to the spot where the ball is going to drop as fast as you can. Stand directly under the ball, so you can see whether it is drifting. Take a step back as you make the catch.

Reach up for the ball. Use both hands.

Left: **Find the ball, then flip off the mask.** *Right:* **Get the glove above your head; use both hands.**

Tagging Runners—Be aggressive when you go after pop-ups. Don't let them intimidate you. The same quality has to characterize your actions in tagging runners barreling for home plate.

If the throw is coming in from right field, position yourself on the third base side of home plate as you wait for it. Don't block the plate. If the throw is coming in from left field, move to the first base side of the plate, keeping in fair territory.

When the ball arrives, glove it, grip it tightly in your bare hand, drop to one knee or both knees on the third base side of the plate, and hold the ball toward the runner, protecting it with your glove. The idea is to make him slide into it.

Forced plays at the plate are less combative. As you take the throw, put your right foot on the plate, making the play like a first baseman.

Remember, it's part of the catcher's responsibility to back up infielders' throws to first base, unless second or third base are occupied. Never, under any circumstances, leave the plate if there is a runner in scoring position.

For successful infield play, be alert as the pitcher winds up.

INFIELD PLAY

Being successful as an infielder takes more than simply knowing how to field the ball and throw it. You should know how to play each batter, where to station yourself. And on each pitch, you should know exactly what you're going to do with the ball if it's hit to you.

As the pitcher goes into his windup, you should be in a semicrouch, your knees slightly bent, your weight forward on the balls of your feet. Keep your hands in front of your knees.

Glue your eyes on the batter. If the ball is hit on the ground to you, be aggressive in fielding it. Move in and glove it at the top of a bounce. Some ground balls will be lashed at you with such power that you won't be able to move in on them, but at least be aggressive in your attitude. No matter what, don't give up any ground.

Get your arms out in front of you as you go for the ball. Be sure to use both hands. Keep low to the ground. You'll be better balanced when you make the throw.

If it's a hard smash, drop to one knee in front of the ball, or field it with your heels together and your knees bent. Even if you don't make a clean pickup, you'll at least block the ball, and you still may have time to make the throw.

When going for a ball that's hit to your left, pivot on your left foot, then step with your right,

Get low for grounders.

crossing it over. Do the reverse when the ball is hit to your right—pivot on your right foot, step with the left. This method provides for the fastest start possible.

Your fielding technique should be such that you are able to make the throw with just one step. If you're throwing to first base, step toward the base

The crossover step

and whip the ball overhand. On a particularly long throw, from deep short, say, you may want to take an extra split second to firmly plant your rear foot, your right foot, before throwing. On short throws, you can often sidearm the ball.

Always have a specific target in mind when you throw. On throws to first base, throw to the mitt target offered by the first baseman. If you're throwing to one of the other bases on a force-out, aim for the fielder's belt buckle. On tag plays, aim lower, about at the fielder's knees.

"With two outs, never make a long throw when a short one will do the job" is a piece of advice you're sure to hear from your coach. Suppose there is a runner on first and the ball is hit to you, the shortstop. Rather than make the long throw to first base, simply toss it to the second baseman for a force-out.

When it's your job to make the tag, dash to the base and straddle it, facing the oncoming runner. When the ball arrives, trap it in the glove's webbing, then drop your gloved hand to the ground in front of the base edge. You want the runner to tag himself out by sliding into the glove. Keep your eye on the man in case you may have to move the glove to the right or left.

The important thing is to let the runner come to you. Don't leave the base and attempt to chase him down.

When you have a runner trapped off base, the

first thing to do is relax. He can't escape if you and your teammates stay cool. If you have the ball, don't throw it needlessly. Instead, take the ball in your bare hand, run right at the man, forcing him to make a decision. If he tries to get to the base you're guarding, tag him out. If he wants to run out of the baseline, let him; he's out, and you don't even have to make a tag. If he runs toward the other base, throw the ball there.

Sometimes there's no need to throw the ball at all. Fake a throw. If the runner takes the fake, you can usually tag him out.

If there is more than one runner on the basepaths, keep aware of what the lead runner is doing, especially if the score is close. Don't sacrifice a run at the cost of an out. If the lead runner is on third and gets too far off the base, whirl and throw to the catcher.

PLAYING FIRST BASE

You don't have to be tall and a left-hander to be a first baseman—but it helps. The taller you are, the bigger the throwing target you offer the other infielders. As for being left-handed, that enables you to make infield throws with greater facility.

You *do*, however, have to be extremely agile, capable of catlike moves. And you *do* have to have what coaches call "good hands," that is, be able to handle any kind of thrown or batted ball, from soft tosses that bounce at your feet to screaming line drives.

A dozen times or more during a game, you'll be on the receiving end of throws to first base. To get in position to take a throw, dash to the base and turn to face the infielder who is going to make the throw. The toe of your right foot (if you're right-handed) should be touching the base. The left foot should be alongside the right.

If the throw comes directly toward you, stride forward with your left foot. Extend the glove as far as you can and make the catch with both hands. On throws that are to your left, your footwork is the same, that is, you stride with your left foot while keeping your right foot on the bag.

But when the throw comes from the right, do the reverse—stride with your right foot and touch the base with your left. It's easy to remember: when the ball is to your left, stride with your left foot;

Reach for the ball; use both hands.

when it's to your right, stride right.

When the ball is hit in your direction, make every effort to get in front of it. Even if you fumble the ball momentarily, you still have a chance of retiring the batter—providing you've stopped the ball.

Work closely with the pitcher on bunts and on balls hit between your playing positions. If there's any doubt as to who is going to field the ball, it's up to you to shout either "Take it!" or "I've got it!"

Sometimes you'll be drawn so far from the base, the pitcher will have to cover. He'll be taking the ball on the run, so lead him with your toss.

With a runner at first, you, as the first baseman, have to keep alert for a possible double play. When a ground ball is hit to you sharply, make the throw to second base, then hustle back to first for the return throw that retires the batter.

If you're playing adjacent to the base when you field a ground ball, simply step on first, then throw to second for the second out. But it all has to be done quickly and deftly; otherwise, you'll never get the runner at second.

Stride with your left foot to take an infielder's throw.

PLAYING SHORTSTOP AND SECOND BASE

Of all the infield positions, that of shortstop is the most demanding. More ground balls and line drives are hit to the shortstop than to any other infielder. He has to range far and wide in catching pop-ups because the foul area beyond the left-field line is usually considered his territory, not the third baseman's. The shortstop often starts double plays or serves as the pivot man.

If sure hands are important to the shortstop, so is a strong arm. The throw he has to make from deep short is the longest infield throw there is.

The second baseman doesn't have quite so varied an assignment. And the throws he makes are considerably shorter than the shortstop's. Still, it takes good hands and an accurate arm to be able to play the position.

The second baseman, because his throws are shorter, plays relatively deep, about on the edge of the outfield grass. Where there's a double-play possibility, he may come in a step or two, but usually no more than that.

Of course, both players adjust their positions to the right or left, depending on whether a leftie or rightie is at the plate. The game situation can also affect where they play; they may move in closer.

The shortstop and second baseman have to work together as a team on many plays. Just how they

Playing shortstop demands good hands, strong arm.

cooperate with one another is detailed in the section of this book titled "Defensive Teamwork."

They also work together to complete double plays. The double play is to the defense what the home run is to the offense. Not only does it have tactical importance, it also has great psychological value, for any time your team completes a double play, the opposition can't help but feel terribly deflated.

Despite these plus factors, keep in mind that the important thing in any double-play attempt is to get the first out. There are few things worse than a double-play try in which no one gets put out.

Almost always the success or failure of the double play hinges upon what happens around second base —the toss to the pivot man at second base, and the pivot man's relay to first. Of course, if you happen to field the ball only a few feet from second base, you can step on the base yourself, and then throw on to first. There's no need to involve the other man.

When you do have to work with a pivot man, feed the ball to him carefully. It's usually a simple underhand toss. Use one hand or two, depending on the situation. The ball should arrive about chin-high.

Success with the toss is more a matter of timing than haste. In other words, don't hurry.

If it's your job to play the role of the pivot man, cross the bag in such a way that you face the thrower squarely. Here again timing is important. If you arrive too early, you may be across the base by the time you get possession of the ball. If you're late, you may get the man at second, but you'll have to rush your throw to first.

There are several ways to execute the pivot. The best methods are those that take you out of the baseline, so you get an unimpeded throw. For a second baseman, a tried and proven method is to step on and across the base as you catch the toss. Step with your left foot striking the bag's edge, and end up on your right foot on the third base side of second. Then step toward first and make the throw. The baserunner will be to your left; you'll have a clear target.

An alternative method is to step back from the base instead of across it. As you make the catch, step on the edge of the bag with your left foot, then step back on your right; throw to first. The problem with this method is that your left foot, your contact foot, is a target for the runner sliding in.

The shortstop can pivot in the same fashion. As he catches the ball, he steps on the base edge with his right foot, lands on his left, pivots, and throws to first.

Or he can pivot on the third base side of second. When he reaches to catch the ball, he touches the base edge with his left foot, pivots on his right foot, then steps toward third and throws.

As a pivot man, keep aware of the situation at first base. It's senseless to make a throw to first if there's no chance of getting the second out.

Making the double play in softball requires more precision than in baseball. This means that plenty of practice is in order.

Double play takes precision teamwork.

PLAYING THIRD BASE

The man at third base may not get as many fielding chances as either the second baseman or shortstop, but he sees a greater variety of balls, ranging from bunt attempts and weak tricklers to sizzling line drives and curving smashes down the foul line. Don't think about playing third base unless you have quick reflexes and a strong throwing arm. And courage.

Usually the third baseman stations himself on a line with the base, moving right or left depending on the hitter. In an obvious bunting situation, he plays in close. He does the same in a tight game, with a runner on third, hoping to make a play at the plate. In the late innings of a close game and with two out, the third baseman usually plays closer to the base than usual in an effort to prevent an extra-base hit down the line.

Coaches want the third baseman to make the fielding play on ground balls hit to his left, which sometimes means he's cutting in front of the shortstop. In such cases, it's the third baseman who has the shorter throw.

But on pop flies, even pop-ups that sail into foul territory, it's the shortstop who makes the catch. Since he plays deeper, he's better able to get positioned for the catch.

If you play third base, you'll have to keep alert for bunts. Don't wait until the ball is heading your way to make your move. Break for the plate as soon as you see the batter face around and put his bat in a position to bunt. Keep in mind that in softball the chances of getting a runner at second base on a sacrifice bunt are very rare.

When possible, field bunts with your bare hand. Whip the ball to first while straightening up.

When there is a runner on second, should you race in to field a bunt, or should you hang back and cover the base? Make the fielding play. The shortstop will cover the bag.

Occasionally you'll have a chance to trigger a double play. The easiest type occurs when there are

The third baseman must often backhand balls hit to his right.

Bunts often must be fielded bare-handed, the throw made from an off-balance position.

runners on first and second base and the ball is smashed directly toward third. All you have to do is glove the ball, step on third, then throw to second for a force-out. When the ball is hit wide of third, go for the double play by way of second.

In taking throws from the outfield with runners on base, concentrate on catching the ball first. Don't let yourself be distracted by the oncoming runner. Straddle the bag; lower your gloved hand so the runner will slide into it.

PLAYING THE OUTFIELD

To be able to play the outfield, and play it well, you have to have good speed, ability as a fielder, and a strong throwing arm. Of these three qualities, coaches regard speed as the most important. If you can start fast and cover distance quickly, you can compensate for an occasional lapse in fielding and throwing.

The center fielder is usually more skilled than either the right or left fielders. Because he has more ground to cover, he has to be the fastest man of the trio. And since many of the throws he makes are particularly long ones, he has to have a strong throwing arm.

However, the player with the strongest arm of all is often positioned in right field. He has to be able to prevent the runner on first base from going all the way to third on a single. This means that he has to have the strength to be able to rifle the ball all the way from right field to third base, an extremely long throw.

Skilled and experienced outfielders seem to know in advance where batted balls are going. They're thus able to catch fly balls that otherwise might fall safely, and cut off ground balls that threaten to become extra-base hits.

One of the key factors in getting a good jump on the ball is your stance. As the pitcher winds up and the batter gets set to swing, you have to be posi-

Outfielder's stance is like that of infielder's. The idea is to be ready to go in any direction.

tioned in such a way that you can move instantly in any direction.

Crouch slightly; lean forward. Put your hands on your knees, or just above them, if this feels comfortable. Spread your feet; concentrate your weight on the balls of your feet.

Watch the pitcher. As soon as he begins his windup, shift your eyes to the hitter. Concentrate on him as he awaits the pitch. Try to figure out from his stance and the way in which he has the bat positioned the direction in which he might hit the ball.

"The biggest problem I have with boys and girls who play the outfield is their lack of attention," says the coach of a Paramus, New Jersey, team. "Sometimes they seem to be daydreaming. So when a ball gets hit their way, they're late getting started."

One way to keep alert in the outfield is to make up your mind to play every ball that's hit—balls to the other fields, foul balls, everything. Like hitting the ball or fielding it cleanly, alertness is a skill that you can acquire.

You can also help yourself to get a jump on the ball by learning to play each batter in accordance with his style and technique, and the game situation. When there's a right-handed batter at the plate, the left and center fielders should move farther to the left than normal, and the right fielder shifts toward center field and a bit closer to the plate. With a left-handed batter at the plate, the reverse happens.

If the batter is small physically and chokes up on the bat, then you can move in a few steps. The same is usually true in the case of a batter who crowds the plate.

The batting order is another clue as to the talents of the individual hitters. The boy or girl who is slotted seventh or eighth in the lineup is not likely to be a power hitter.

Sometimes the ball-strike count furnishes a tip-off on where to play a batter. When the count is no balls, two strikes or one ball, two strikes, the man at the plate is almost surely to be swinging freely, trying for an extra-base hit. The outfielders back up a step or two. But any time there are two strikes on the batter, the outfielders move in. They know the batter is merely going to be trying to meet the ball, not swing away.

The game situation can also help determine where you play. If play is in the late innings and a double or triple will hurt your team, then you might play deeper than normal. But suppose it's the seventh inning, and the winning run is on second base. Then you would play much closer to the infield in order to be able to throw out the baserunner at the plate. It's a risk, of course, but most managers want their outfielders to take it.

Keep an eye on the bench in crucial situations. Your manager may want to change your positioning.

The quickest way to move to either your right or left for a batted ball is to begin with what is known as a crossover step. If you have to go to your left, cross your right leg over your left leg and push off on your left foot. Do the reverse when you have to go back for it; don't pedal back, turn and go. Race to the spot when you think the ball is going to come down, checking its flight over your shoulder as you go.

Coaches want their outfielders to play as close to the infield as they possibly can in order to catch balls that might otherwise drop in for base hits. But if you can't go back quickly, you won't be able to play in close.

If you're playing on a field where there is an outfield fence, and you have to go deep to get a fly ball, it's usually best to turn and run to the fence as fast as you can, watching the ball as you go. When you reach the fence, come back and make the catch. Your awareness of where the fence is situated will help to prevent a collision—and the injury that can result.

Making the Catch—Catch every fly ball with two hands. There is no rule more important. Use a long-fingered glove with a good deal of webbing and a deep pocket. Learn to catch the ball in the webbing.

Using both hands is not only the more reliable way to catch, it's the more efficient way, too. Doing so means that you'll have your throwing hand on the ball as you make the catch, and this will enable you to get rid of the ball quickly.

Be relaxed as you make the catch. You should have what coaches call "soft" hands.

Make the catch at least head-high.

Keep your arms extended. When the ball strikes your glove, let your hands, wrists, and arms absorb the impact.

If there is any "secret" to making catches in the outfield, it has to do with following the ball. From the moment the ball leaves the bat until it hits into your glove, your eyes should be glued to it. This tip won't help you, however, if you don't practice. Only by practicing will you be able to develop the skill to judge the ball's flight and react instantly to it.

On any routine fly ball, make the catch at about eye level, or slightly higher. Keep the glove well above your head, but don't position it in such a way that it's going to block your view of the ball. The fingers of the glove should point upward.

When you become experienced, learn to position the glove more toward your throwing side as you wait to make the catch. And get your body in position to make the throw, putting your left foot ahead of your right (if you're a right-hander).

On a low-hit ball, position the glove so that the fingers point down. Coaches call the belt the dividing line; in catching balls above belt level, the glove fingers should point up. Below belt level, they should point down.

The most difficult ball for you to catch is likely to be the line drive that's hit straight at you. As it comes off the bat, it's difficult to judge the speed of the ball and whether it's rising or sinking. You could charge in to make the catch, only to have the ball

Make the catch like this when the ball is below belt level.

soar over your head. The best thing to do is wait a split second before making your move. It's almost always wiser to play it safe, catching the ball after it bounces once. Shoestring catches are for professionals.

Communication between outfielders is of vital importance. As soon as you are sure you can make the catch, yell out, "I've got it! I've got it!" Don't be afraid to keep repeating it.

When a teammate calls for the ball, always answer him. Shout out "Take it! Take it!" Without this kind of dialogue, outfield collisions can occur.

Once you've called for a ball, heard the other fielder respond, and started for it, it's yours no matter where it happens to go. Take the case of a towering pop hit just past the infield. A strong wind may carry the ball back toward home plate. You, the outfielder, may wind up pursuing the ball in territory that's normally covered by the shortstop or second baseman. But it's still your ball; you called for it. Stay with it all the way.

Outfielders should yell instructions to one another at every opportunity. If you're playing on a fenced-in field, and one of your teammates is pursuing a long fly ball, let him know whether the fence presents a hazard. A shout of "Lots of room! Take it!" can be a big help.

It's especially difficult catching fly balls hit into the sun. Use sunglasses, not the ordinary kind, but the special "flip-down" glasses sold in sporting goods stores. These have hinged lenses. They are worn with the lenses in a raised position until the ball is hit your way. When you tap the peak of your cap, the lenses snap down to screen out the sun's glare. Such glasses have adjustable elastic headbands to keep them securely in place.

Flip-down sunglasses can be a big help.

Don't wait until you're in a game to try out the glasses. Use them in practice sessions until you can flip down the lenses automatically.

If you're playing on a sunny day and you don't have sunglasses, use your glove as a sunshade. As the ball is pitched, hold your glove up above your face so as to block out the sun.

Fielding Grounders—How you play a ground ball often depends on the game situation. If play is in a late inning and the tieing or winning run is on second base, and the ball is laced through the infield, you must charge in, glove the ball, then get rid of it quickly, hopefully cutting off the run. In other words, you handle the ball in much the same way as an infielder would.

But when no quick throw is necessary, the idea is to play the ball safely. Drop one knee to the ground—your right knee if you're right-handed—so as to block the ball should it happen to elude your glove.

In cases where you have to charge in and make a quick throw, don't try to scoop up the ball with one hand. Use both hands. Not only are you less likely to fumble the ball, but you'll be able to get into your throwing position faster.

Coaches say that young players make more errors on grounders than they do on fly balls. If you need practice in this department, work out with the infielders.

Fly balls and ground balls that rip through the

Don't wait for the ground balls to come to you.

Always use both hands.

infield aren't the only responsibilities that outfielders have. They also must back up the infielders and other outfielders whenever they can on both thrown and batted balls.

The right fielder should back up first base on bunt attempts or pick-off attempts, or on any other plays made there. The left fielder should do the same as concerns third base. Plays at second base should be backed up by the center fielder.

Outfield Throws—Accuracy is what to strive for when making a throw from the outfield. If the ball is off target in a critical situation, it can prove very costly to your team.

One way to attain accuracy is by using an overhand delivery when you throw. Bring the ball back, then whip it forward, releasing it above the level of your head. What you should avoid is the sidearm throw, which can cause the ball to hook or curve. Throwing overhand imparts backspin to the ball and this helps to keep it on course. You can increase the amount of backspin by gripping the ball across the seams as you throw.

Keep the throw low. A well-thrown ball that travels in a straight line and close to the ground, even if it bounces, will get to the target faster than a ball that arcs high in the air.

Quite often your target will be a relay man, one of the infielders who comes out onto the outfield grass to take your throw and rifles it to third base or home plate. Often two short throws will reach the base faster than one long one.

This is another reason to keep the ball low. A high throw is likely to go over the relay man's head. Aim to hit him in the chest with the ball.

Usually you'll be throwing, not to a relay man, but to an infielder at one of the bases. Know where you're going to throw before the ball arrives. Throw to the base ahead of the runner. Again, keep the ball low, aiming for the infielder's knees.

If you're playing on a chilly day, take plenty of time warming up your throwing arm. Before the game throw to a teammate. Start at a distance of 20 or 30 feet and gradually move back. Keep the arm warm by throwing before each inning begins; throw to one of your teammates in the outfield.

Outfielder's throw is overhand, never sidearm. Be sure to follow through.

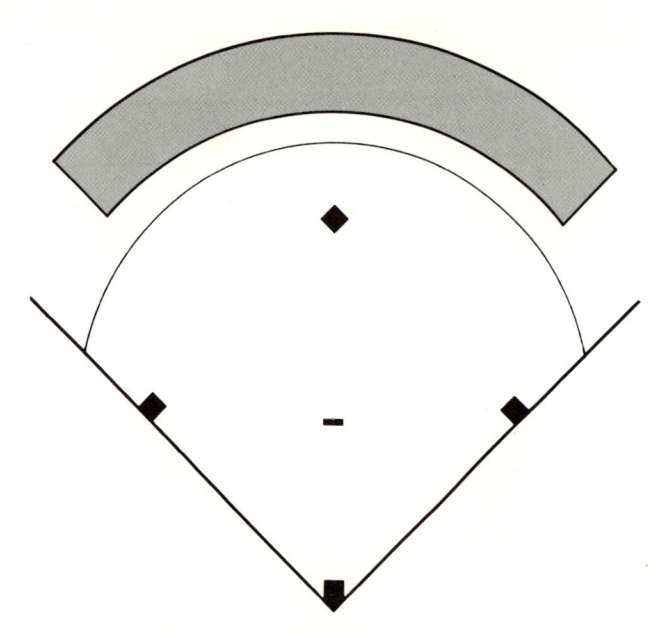

Area covered by the short fielder

THE SHORT FIELDER

In slow-pitch softball, one playing position is wholly unique; it's that of short fielder.

The player who fills this position must combine many of the skills of the infielders and outfielders. He has to be adept at scooping up ground balls and throwing quickly, because occasionally he can throw out a runner at second base or first. He also has to be sure-handed in catching fly balls. He is sometimes called the shortstop of the outfield.

From his playing position behind second base, the short fielder gloves down line drives that would ordinarily land in short center field, and he gathers in pop flies which, in baseball, would be Texas League singles. He seldom serves as a relay man, however; that's a job handled by either the shortstop or second baseman.

More than any other defensive player, the short fielder has to know the opposition batters, know where they're going to hit the ball and how hard. Stationed about 10 feet in back of second base, he can range 20 to 30 feet to his right or left. That gives him a coverage area that's almost as big as an outfielder's. Knowing precisely where to play within that is vital to his success.

When there's a power hitter at the plate, the short fielder may move deep into the outfield, becoming a fourth outfielder. The team will then have a left fielder, a left center fielder, a right center fielder (the short fielder), and a right fielder.

① Pitcher
② Catcher
③ First Baseman
④ Second Baseman
⑤ Third Baseman
⑥ Shortstop
⑦ Left Fielder
⑧ Center Fielder
⑨ Right Fielder
⑩ Short Fielder
Ⓧ Base Runner
o o o Batted Ball
- - - - Thrown Ball

Key to Diagrams

DEFENSIVE TEAMWORK

While the talent you bring to your position is important, you and the other members of your team can't hope for success unless you learn to blend your skills into a smooth working unit. This section is meant to help you determine your responsibilities in each of a number of typical game situations.

Follow the diagrams and the comments about them. The key at left indicates the various positions by numbers, with an X for the base runner. A batted ball is shown with a dotted line. A thrown ball is indicated by a broken line. The first diagram, for a bunt defense with a runner on first, is on the next page.

Bunt Defense with a Runner on First—For participants as well as spectators, this is always an exciting play. The third baseman (5), once he knows the bunt is coming, stations himself about a third of the way down the line. The first baseman (3) plays in, too, but not quite so far. Both men, along with the pitcher (1), charge plateward as the ball is released.

The second baseman (4) dashes over to cover first. The shortstop (6) covers second.

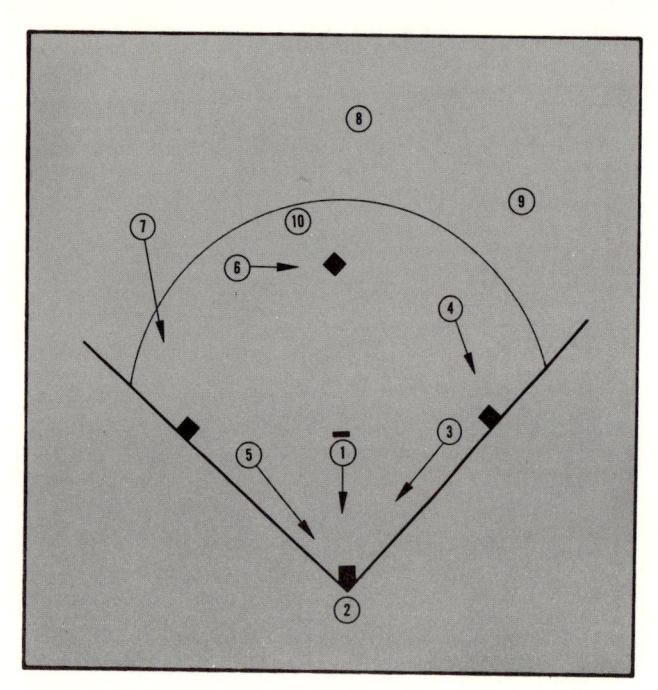

"plink"—of the bat. If it's a routine hit, that is, not too deep, the left fielder (7) simply whips the ball to second base, the second baseman (4) covering.

Does the left fielder have a chance for a put-out at second? If the runner is slow afoot, the possibility exists, but it happens only rarely.

The shortstop (6) hurries out onto the outfield grass to station himself between the left fielder and the second baseman, thus giving the fielder a target at which to throw. The pitcher (1) backs up second base.

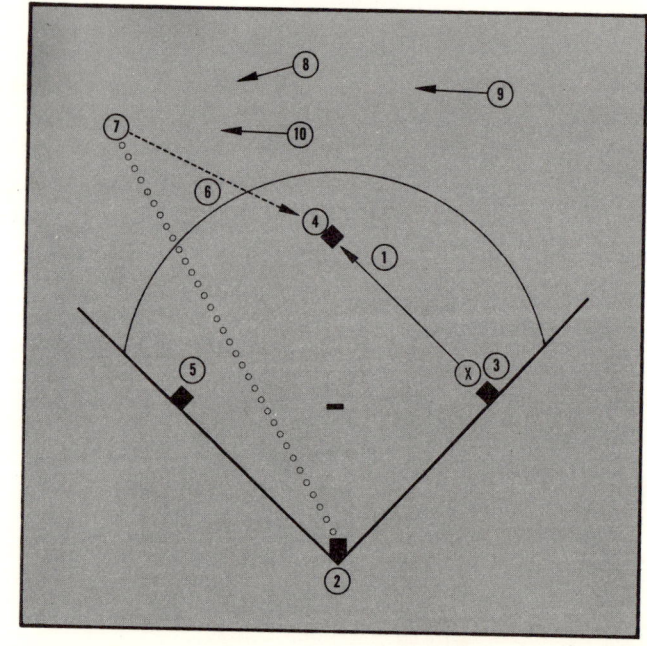

The short fielder (10) backs up second base. The left fielder (7) has to be alert for a play at third.

What the batter tries to do is to push the ball past the pitcher, that is, to his left or right. If he's not successful, it's a certain out.

Single to Left Field with a Runner on First Base—This happens so frequently during a game that most players react automatically to the crack—or

Single to Left Field with a Runner on Second Base—The left fielder (7) can never handle this play in routine fashion. He has to be thinking. If the ball isn't hit too deeply, he makes the play into second base, the second baseman (4) taking his throw.

But if the ball is well hit, the left fielder has to keep a watchful eye on the runner on second, because he's going to be flying for home plate. If the

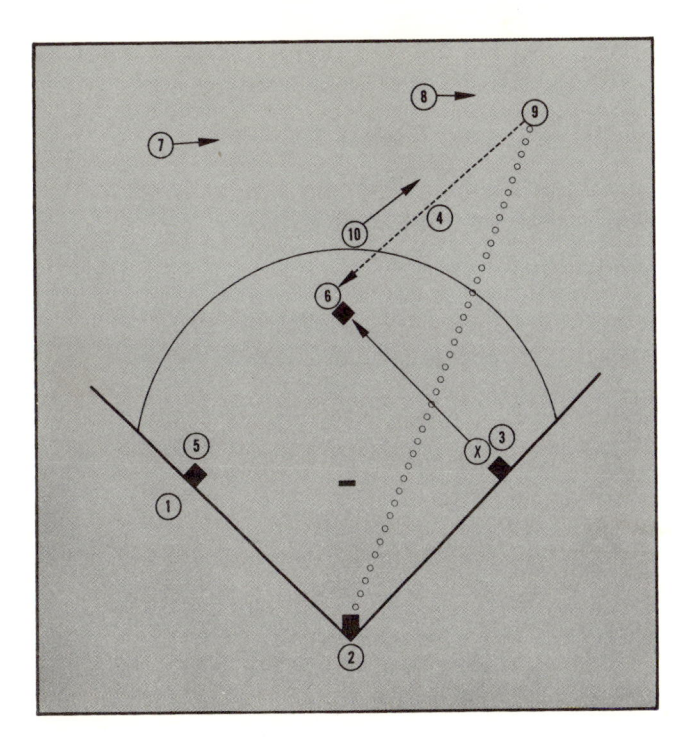

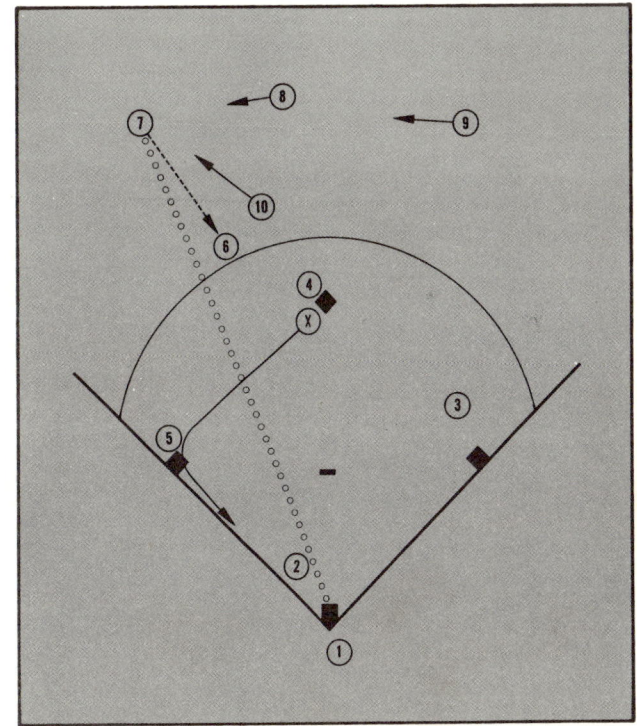

Single to Right Field with a Runner on First Base—With a left-handed batter at the plate and the previous batter having singled, this is the situation that can result. This time the shortstop (6) covers second base, taking the throw from the right fielder (9). The second baseman (4) lines up between the outfielder making the throw and second base. The pitcher (1) backs up third base, in case there's a play there.

59

runner rounds third and looks like he might be heading for the plate, as shown here, the throw goes to the shortstop (6), who will relay to the catcher (2). The pitcher (1) backs up at home plate.

Single to Right Field with a Runner on Second Base—The pressure is on the right fielder (9) in this situation. His throw goes to second base, the shortstop (6) covering. But he has to be cautious, eyeing the runner; he may have a play at home. The ball has to be fielded cleanly, crisply, and rifled back to the infield.

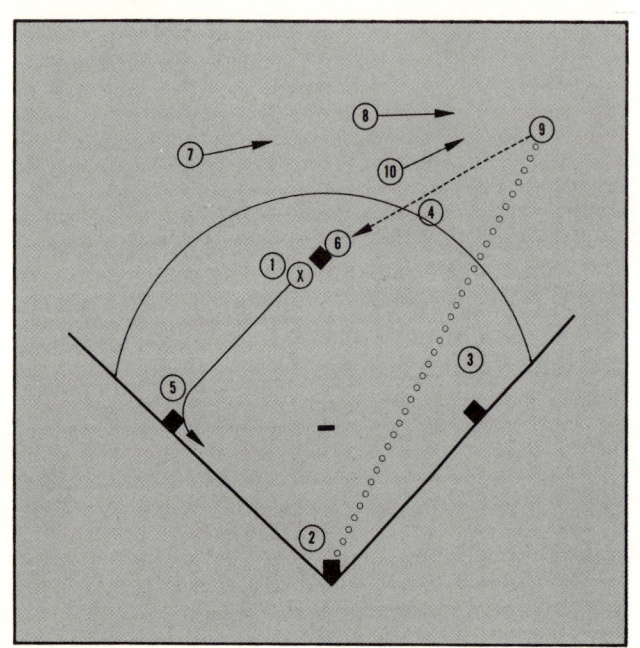

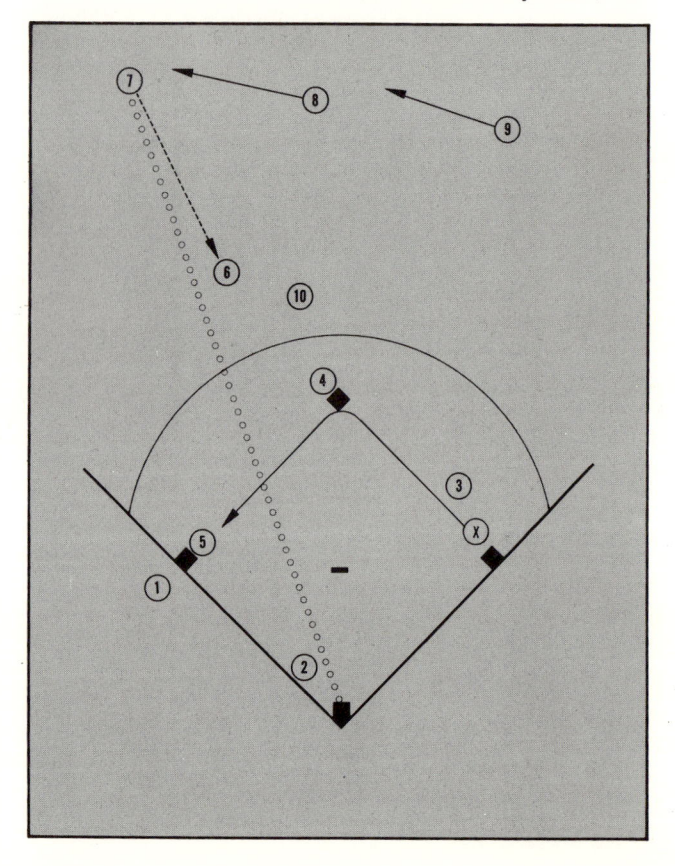

Extra-base Hit to Left Field with a Runner on First Base—The defense has to concede that the runner on first is going to reach third in this situation. But will he score? It depends; it depends on how far the ball is hit and how quickly the left fielder (7) can throw the ball to the relay man, the shortstop (6). He's the defensive player who is under the most pressure. As the relay man, it's up to him to decide whether to make the play at home plate or try to get the runner who will be coming into second.

If it's a close game, the relay man's chief worry is the lead runner. The pitcher backs up at third base.

Extra-base Hit to Right Field with a Runner on First Base—It's almost certain that the baserunner will make it safely to the plate in this situation. After the right fielder (9) retrieves the ball, he throws to the second baseman (4), the relay man. If it's a long drive, a potential triple, the second baseman positions himself on a line between third base and the outfielder (as shown here), and rifles the ball to the third baseman (5). The pitcher (1) has to hurry over to back up third.

The catcher remains at the plate, no matter where the ball goes.

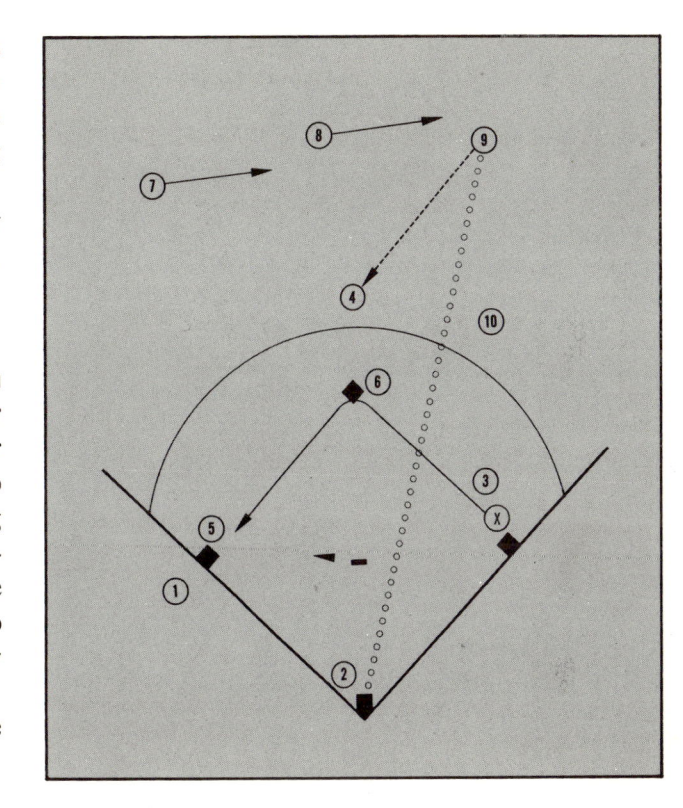

61

Should he keep going or stop? It's up to the coach to decide.

HOW TO COACH

When your team is at bat, your manager may ask you to coach at either first or third base. Look upon it as an opportunity to contribute to your team's offense. In a close game, a coach's decision can be what tips the scales in your team's favor.

You serve as a one-man information center any time you're coaching. Keep the runners informed as to the count, the number of outs, and the various play possibilities that are at hand. Tell them where the infielders and outfielders are playing.

Talk to the runner on first or third between pitches. Should he be playing it safe or running all-out no matter what? You should know the throwing ability of each of the outfielders and the catcher, and should advise the runner accordingly. In the case of a runner on second, yell and use hand signals to keep him informed.

Instructing runners as to whether they should tag up is one of your chief responsibilities. The runner on third should tag up whenever a ball is hit into the air. It's up to you to judge whether he should go all the way home or merely fake going, so as to draw a throw. Yell out your instructions loudly and clearly. You should sound like a Marine drill sergeant.

When there are no outs, have a runner on first or second base tag up on any long fly ball. If there is a question as to whether the ball is going to be caught, have the runner go at least far enough to draw a throw.

You also have responsibilities as a traffic cop. When coaching at third base, signal the oncoming runner whether he should slide or stay erect. For a slide, give him a palms-down signal. Push your palms toward the runner when you want him to stay up. Always get into the runner's line of vision when you signal.

When you want the runner to round third and keep going, don't let there be any doubt about it. Wave him on and shout "Go! Go! Go!" Run with him down the line so that you can keep him informed until the very last second.

Some teams use a signal system for bunts and steals, with the third base coach conveying signals from the manager on the bench to the runner and batter. The signal itself is easy to read. The coach may touch the peak of his cap, pull at an ear, hitch up his trousers, fold his arms—almost anything. What makes it confusing to the opposition is that he does all of these things, and more, in rapid sequence. Only one of the signals is the real signal. The others are camouflage.

If you have any doubt that a runner or the batter has missed a signal, immediately call time out and have a private conference with the man.

Besides the duties outlined above, a coach is also a cheerleader. Yell, whistle, clap your hands; do all you can to keep runners alert and the hitter encouraged.

Coaching signals

GLOSSARY

AMATEUR SOFTBALL ASSOCIATION (ASA)—Softball's governing body; the ASA conducts national tournaments, provides the organizational structure for local competition, promotes junior leagues and tournaments, and sponsors instruction clinics for players, coaches, and umpires.

BASEPATH—An imaginary line 3 feet to either side of a direct line between the bases.

BATTER'S BOX—The area—3 feet by 7 feet—to which the batter is restricted during his turn at the plate.

CHANGE-UP—A slow pitch thrown with the same motion as a fast one.

CHOKE; CHOKE-UP—To grip the bat several inches from the knob end.

DRAG BUNT—A surprise bunt pushed down a baseline or between infielders in a base hit attempt.

FAST-PITCH—That type of softball in which the pitcher may use any type of underhand delivery he desires, providing he does not make more than one revolution of the arm as he winds up and releases the ball. There are nine members to a team. The pitcher stands 40 feet from home plate (in most junior competition) and the bases are 60 feet apart.

FORCE-OUT—Putting a runner out by tagging the base to which he must advance.

HOOK SLIDE—A slide in which the runner leans his upper body away from the base while "hooking" it with one foot.

INTERNATIONAL SOFTBALL FEDERATION—The international governing body of softball. Among its goals are to standardize playing rules and regulations among member nations and to establish softball as an Olympic sport.

ON DECK—Waiting to take one's turn at bat as the next hitter.

PITCHER'S PLATE—The oblong piece of hard rubber upon which the pitcher pivots as he delivers the ball; also known as the pitcher's rubber.

PIVOT MAN—On a double play, the infielder who receives a fielded ball at second base, and relays it to first base for the second out.

RELAY MAN—The infielder—almost always the shortstop or second baseman—who takes the throw from the outfield, and throws it on to another infielder or the catcher.

SACRIFICE BUNT—A bunted ball struck with less than two out, which is meant to advance a runner or runners; the batter is retired at first base.

SACRIFICE FLY—A fair fly ball struck with less than two outs, which serves to advance a runner or runners.

SHORT FIELDER—In slow-pitch softball, a tenth player who is stationed on the outfield grass behind second base or used as a fourth outfielder.

SLOW-PITCH—That type of softball in which the ball must be pitched at moderate speed, and so that it arches from 3 to 10 feet on its way to the batter. There are ten members to a team. The pitcher stands 40 feet from home plate (in most junior competition) and the bases are 60 feet apart. Bunting and base stealing are not permitted.

SQUEEZE—A play in which the runner breaks from third with the pitch, and the batter bunts the ball to enable the runner to score.

STRIKE ZONE—The space over home plate between the batter's armpits and the tops of his knees.

TAG UP—On a fly ball, to return and touch the base with one foot before running to the next base or to home plate.